What Happens When I Burp?

By Jaden Troiano

Gareth Stevens
Publishing

Please visit our website, www.garethstevens.com. For a free color catalog of all our high-quality books, call toll free 1-800-542-2595 or fax 1-877-542-2596.

Library of Congress Cataloging-in-Publication Data

Troiano, Jaden.
What happens when I burp? / by Jaden Troiano.
   p. cm. — (My body does strange stuff!)
Includes index.
ISBN 978-1-4824-0255-1 (pbk.)
ISBN 978-1-4824-0256-8 (6-pack)
ISBN 978-1-4824-0252-0 (library binding)
1. Digestion — Juvenile literature. 2. Digestive organs — Juvenile literature. 3. Belching — Juvenile literature. I. Title.
QP145.T76 2014
612.3—dc23

Published in 2014 by
Gareth Stevens Publishing
111 East 14th Street, Suite 349
New York, NY 10003

Designer: Michael J. Flynn
Editor: Greg Roza

Photo credits: Cover, p. 1 Rob Lewine/Getty Images; p. 5 Julija Sapic/Shutterstock.com; p. 7 Image Source/Zero Creatives/Getty Images; p. 9 Pavel L Photo and Video/Shutterstock.com; p. 11 Sebastian Kaulitzki/Shutterstock.com; p. 12 Suzanne Tucker/Shutterstock.com; p. 15 Blamp/Shutterstock.com; p. 17 sunabesyou/Shutterstock.com; p. 19 Diego Cervo/Shutterstock.com; p. 21 Ruud Morijn Photographer/Shutterstock.com.

Printed in the United States of America

CPSIA compliance information: Batch #CW14GS: For further information contact Gareth Stevens, New York, New York at 1-800-542-2595.

Contents

Boldface words appear in the glossary.

Excuse Me!

Everybody burps. Some people try to hide them. Others love to burp out loud. Some people think burping is rude, but others find it funny. Sometimes we even surprise ourselves with a burp! But why do we do it? Read on to find out!

Building Burps

A burp starts when we swallow air while eating or drinking. This air builds up in the stomach, or tummy, but soon it wants to come out. The air moves out of the stomach, up a tube called the esophagus (ih-SAH-fuh-guhs), and out of the mouth.

Eating or drinking too fast is one of the most common causes of burping. Spicy foods are known to cause burping, and so are fatty foods. You also swallow a lot of air when you chew gum, which can lead to burping.

In and Out

When you swallow, **muscles** in your esophagus push food and air down to your stomach. Once there, **stomach acid** breaks down the food, which can create more gas. All that gas can actually make you feel fuller than you really are.

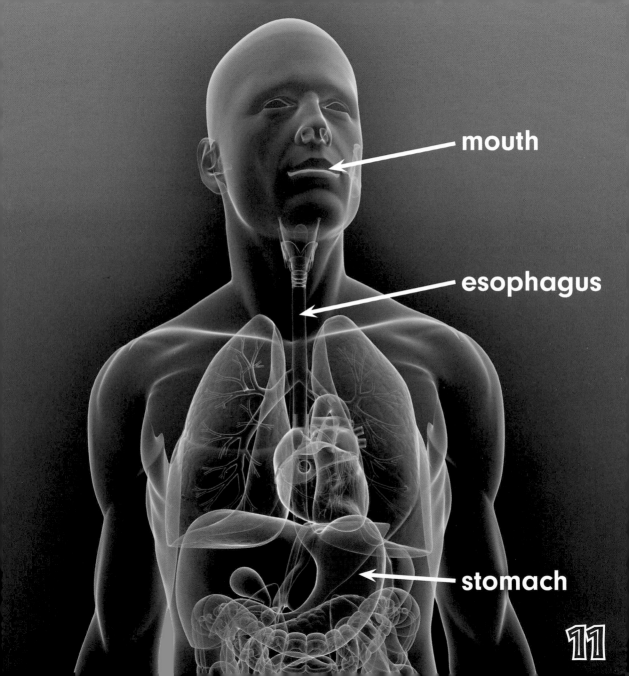

mouth

esophagus

stomach

11

As you eat, gas builds up in your stomach. Soon, the stomach wants to get rid of that gas. It forces the gas up the esophagus and out of your mouth as a burp. Suddenly you feel like you can eat a little more!

That Burping Sound

When you swallow, the upper end of the esophagus opens to let food in. It remains closed until you swallow again. When you burp, air from your stomach is forced through the upper end. This is what causes the sound when you burp.

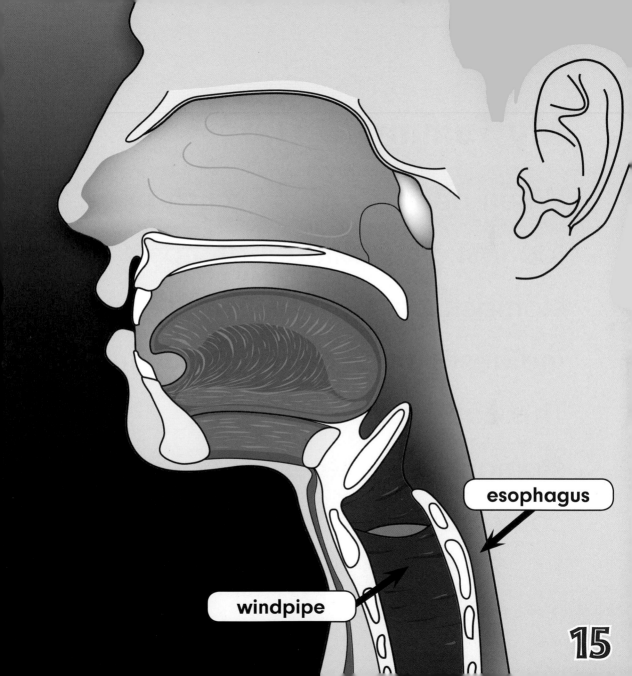

esophagus

windpipe

15

My Tummy Hurts!

When people eat too much or too fast, they can get an upset stomach. This is also called indigestion (ihn-duh-JEHS-chuhn). This can cause pain in the stomach and the esophagus. It can also cause burping.

Some **medicines** help get rid of indigestion, and some even help you burp the pain away! A bicarbonate (by-KAHR-buh-nuht) is a medicine that **reduces** stomach acid. It may be added to water, which creates a lot of bubbles. This helps you burp and eases indigestion.

Animal Burps

Dogs burp after eating a meal too quickly. Many kinds of cattle burp, too. Cow burps contain a gas called **methane**. This gas is bad for the **environment**. Scientists are looking for ways to control cow burps!

Glossary

environment: the natural world around us

medicine: a drug taken to make a sick person well

methane: a colorless, odorless gas that burns easily

muscle: one of the parts of the body that allow movement

reduce: to make less

stomach acid: a liquid in the stomach that breaks down food. Too much stomach acid can cause indigestion.

For More Information

Books

Barraclough, Sue. *The Digestive System: What Makes Me Burp?* Chicago, IL: Heinemann Library, 2008.

Kenah, Katharine. *Fascinating! Human Bodies.* Greensboro, NC: Spectrum, 2013.

Ripley Entertainment. *Burp! Crazy Human Body Stories.* New York, NY: Scholastic, 2011.

Websites

Indigestion
kidshealth.org/kid/ill_injure/aches/indigestion.html
Read more about indigestion, what causes it, and how to cure it.

Why Do I Burp?
kidshealth.org/kid/talk/yucky/burp.html
Learn more about burping.

Index